From the Heart

From the Heart

Poetic Reflections on Growing Old in Maine

KEN NYE

Illustrated by Susan Gilbert

Freeport, Maine

2007

Published by TJMF Publishing

Library of Congress Control Number: 2007902803

ISBN
0-9789705-3-5
978-0-9789705-3-6

Copyright © 2007 by TJMF Publishing

Illustrations Copyright © 2007 by Susan Gilbert

Printed in the United States of America
by Publisher Graphics
May, 2007

Cover photo: The Nye Home in Freeport

For my family,
five generations in my lifetime spanning three centuries (possibly four), from
my Grandma Cook, born in 1888 and who, when I was in bed with the
chicken pox, brought me a chicken salad sandwich made with all the
parts of the chicken, including gristle and fat (I waited until she left
my sickroom and then spit it out the window) to my granddaughters,
born in the 1990's and who may live into the 22nd century, who
already use devices about which I have no understanding and
use vocabulary words which I have never heard.

And

always for Ann, the keeper of my heart, no matter what its age.

WHO BESTOWS THE TITLE "POET"?

Who bestows the title "poet"?
Other poets? Unknown critics?
Men with titles? Longer names?
Who decides my poem is worthy?
Judges, teachers, family, spouse?

Things created have intention
built in structure,
rhythm,
rhyme.
Images and metaphors, ("conceits" they call them)
move the meaning,
showing "this" and meaning "that."
But if the reader doesn't get it,
if the reader is left numb,
the image didn't do it,
and the poem remains unsung.
In that case,
the title "poet"'s a misnomer,
the poem's intention still unclear.

But if the poem moves the reader—
if the reader nods in recognition
of feelings shared and thoughts endorsed,
if the poem breathes of truth and candor,
pulls up feelings never spoken,
throws a light on thoughts long buried,
or tells a story all can see,
the poem will change the reader
and the poet's intentions will succeed.

Who bestows the title "poet"?
Those who read the thing created.
Those who weigh it with their lives.

Ken Nye

TABLE OF CONTENTS

Ponderings

Growing Old Together

Conclusions

PREFACE

Just a couple of very short years ago I was invited to join a poetry site called emergingpoets.net, and as my old mentor, Howard Starks would have said, "My life thereafter was a different thing."

Among the many pleasant things and people I found there was an unbelievably gifted Yankee poet by the name of Ken Nye. His easy conversational narrative poems made me feel instantly connected. I saw his world. I felt his presence in that world, and I was moved by his words. It didn't even seem odd to me that an Okie descending from Cowboys and Indians would be so struck by a Northerner. I mean, the part of Oklahoma from where I hail is known as "Little Dixie"; for Heaven sakes, how could this happen? But it *did* happen.

Our common ground far outweighed any geographical boundaries. We both had a great set of parents and worshipped them in our writing. We had strong family ties. We both loved our dogs and valued them as friends. When he wrote of Monhegan Island and his farm in rural Maine, I saw Oklahoma's rolling hills and valleys and my own parents' little place above the Red. When he wrote about the people and the natural world surrounding him, it felt like home to me. That's a rare talent in a writer and the mark of a great one. When a poet can do what Ken does with his words, put the reader right there beside him, he can transform the reader, move him, make him a part of the work.

Ken was the first featured poet at emergingpoets, the first solo author to be published by TJMF publishing, and his book, *Searching For The Spring*, became the benchmark for those of us who would follow. My wife and I were allowed the privilege of meeting Ken and his lovely wife, Ann, this October in Memphis at The Southern Festival of Books, and the man who had seemed like a friend through cyberspace became a tangible handshake and a real friend standing right there before me.

I see a rebirth of poetry coming in this nation. There are a number of new poets rising and many of them are rising from this publishing site, a list too long to name them all, but I think I can say we look at Ken as the one who has blazed the trail, set the standard. I think all the emergingpoets writers look at his work and how it effects his readers not only as confirming his place among modern poets, but as opening a world of possibilities for all poets.

Everything Ken's poetry said he was turned out to be true. His writing speaks of family, a love of Maine and this country, a belief that nature is a thing of beauty and wonder, and the idea that man is good and can be better. And that's Ken; what you see is what you get, honest, compassionate, intelligent, just like his poetry. The only flaw I've been able to find in the man is his loyalty to the Boston Red Sox, but then I guess no one is perfect. I jest, of course, but being a diehard New York Yankee fan, I can honestly say I would still love Ken Nye even if he were a Dodger fan.

I count the opportunity to write this preface among my highest honors as a writer. His work is real. His voice is real. I have read few writers who have touched me with their words like Ken has: Ted Kooser, Robinson Jeffers, James Dickey, Ron Buck, Donna Timney, Lynn Doiron and Howard Starks. I'm certain Ken and a small host of others know how big a compliment I pay personally with the inclusion of that last name. Howard opened the door to poetry for me thirty years ago, and now Ken has helped to reopen it, reawaken something in all our work.

In the opening of this new collection, Ken asks, "Who bestows the title *Poet?*" and he rightly concludes, "Those who read the thing created. / Those who weigh it with their lives." Therefore, I, as one voice among a multitude of voices, proclaim Ken Nye "Poet," and after readers have finished with this new effort by Mr. Nye that multitude will grow exponentially, for it is as magnificent an achievement as was his first book.

Ron Wallace
Durant, Oklahoma
November, 2006

INTRODUCTION

After the success of his *Searching for the Spring* collection, Ken Nye has compiled a larger, more intense volume in *From the Heart*. It is the soul of a man exploring his thoughts on and his relationships to a universe of people, animals, life's joys, and the acceptance of inevitable death. It is truly a compilation of a man's soul, uplifting, humorous, loving, appreciative of the present, and, as well, lovingly cognizant of his past.

The humor begins with his dedication, "For my Family," in which he relates his Grandmother Cook's recipe for coping with chicken pox. It continues through to a much later poem titled "Singing in the Shower," a testament of strength, courage, and joy.

This collection is Everyman, speaking for all. Time and again, as I read, my mind would recognize and mutter, "I have been in a similar place," "I know that feeling, that delight," I do the very same thing." Most importantly, "I FEEL the same way."

And it is the FEELING aroused and the pictures in the reader's mind that are so important here. To FEEL connected to one's family and friends, to the woods, animals and water, the spiritual universe: "... deer lingering in the orchard, hoping to find just one more apple still clinging to a lower branch." Or "there are times when I simply wander in the woods, following the sounds of music from iced over stream beds to cedar waxwings in tree tops . . ." And the Mahoosic Range, "one mountain silhouetted behind another . . . like a scene in my old Viewmaster." And, again, ". . . a magnificent male coyote . . . his demeanor spoke of responsibilities and decisions to be made."

In "Hymns of Joy," the singing rhythm of Walt Whitman is echoed by Nye's "I heard a whippoorwill last night/ sing his wonder of the world./The forest hushed, /caught in the spell /conjured by the whippoorwill." Throughout this collection, but especially in the section "America the Beautiful," the grandiose wonder and the singing of this continent's geography are part and parcel of Utah's Zion Canyon, of Nebraska's Niobrara River. And in the East, a clapboard church built by the strong, singing hands of neighbors during our agrarian period.

Closer to home, to Nye's heart, the sections on "Friends and

Family" and "Growing Old Together" are his love poems, intimate yet universal, tender yet realistic, poignant yet sturdy. And each, moving, touching.

From the Heart is a collection to linger with, a companionship with Nature and with the nature in each of us. In all of its melodies, it a song of wonder for us all.

Burt deFrees
North Rumford, Maine

FOREWORD

I struggled coming up with a title for this collection of poems. I experimented with a number of titles and ways to organize the poems, but, because almost all of them flow from events in my life, the collection does not follow a particular theme but rather functions as a journal or memoir. And that being the case, they are quite personal.

However, they are also somewhat universal. My life as a 64 year-old is probably not very different from the lives of millions of other 64 year-olds. We have aging parents. children who are no longer children, grandchildren who are living in a world very different from the one in which we grew up. Our bodies are wearing out. We are on the downhill part of life's mountain climb. Many, like me, are retired. So I think the poems in here will resonate with others who are living the same issues and probably feeling the same emotions as I.

Actually, since I began writing poetry a little over three years ago, I have concluded that, to be effective, a poem must be personal. It has to come from the heart of the poet and, if it works, it goes to the heart of the reader. Consequently, after much angst and a number of false starts, I settled on "From the Heart," even though it has the ring of a cliché.

I was sorely tempted to use the poem "Making Love" from my first book as the title poem of this collection because it seemed to say simply in its title what I think this new book is all about. But to title this collection "Making Love" would have misled many potential book shoppers, turning some people off because they would have assumed the poetry within was steamy, and, for the same reason, turning some people on, only to find out later that they had been duped. To be honest, when I put the title on the poem "Making Love," I intentionally played on our culture's obsession with sex, using a title that would lead people to think that Ken Nye might actually have written a steamy poem, only to find out that he was simply talking about the connection between the hearts of two people.

But, had I entitled this book "Making Love," it would not have been to titillate readers. Actually, the poem itself points out that love need not be steamy. As a matter of fact, it rarely is. But, although we don't always recognize the role of love in our everyday lives, it is central to our human experience. And, because this collection of poems is reflective of the day-to-day events in my life, although there is no physical passion in this collection, there is love everywhere you look.

As I have gotten older, it has become more and more clear to me that, using a cliché put to music, "love makes the world go 'round." Actually I have come to believe that it not only makes the world go 'round, it is the primal source of creative power in the universe, and that this life-giving and sustaining power manifests itself in countless ways. One is in the experience that is known to most human beings as "falling in love." Usually, when two people fall in love, especially if they are young, accompanying the emotional and psychological comfort they feel when with each other is the urge to become physically intimate. Kahill Gibran says that children are the result of "life longing for itself." When two people become involved in a physical relationship, they are responding to the creative aspect of "Love" (with a capital "L"). We shouldn't be surprised when young lovers want to sleep over.

But, sadly our culture has become obsessed with satisfying this natural urge, creating an environment in which "love" is construed to be sex and nothing more. There is so much sex on television, in the theater, in popular and rock music, in virtually every sector of living, that many young men and women become inured to the magic of a truly loving relationship. They never come to understand that real, lasting love is the result of much more than chemistry.

My father said once, "The greatest thing a man can do for his children is to love their mother." I know that this has sexist overtones, but my dad was raised in the early part of the 20th century and lived the man's role as prescribed by that era, so this quote reflects that paradigm. But if you put aside (or ignore) the dated wording and dig for an understanding of what he was talking about, you will hear the implication that love is not simply the spontaneous combustion of chemicals in the hearts of two star-crossed lovers. I think my dad would have conceded that chemistry is probably involved in the genesis of a loving relationship, but he seemed to imply that somewhere in the mysterious act of loving another person there is a role for conscious decision making and commitment. And that is why I am focusing on "Making Love."

We are not little mechanical things wound up at birth and placed on the table of life for some godlike creator to chuckle over as we move and interact in preprogrammed lives. We are born with natural tendencies, but we are also born with brains and hearts that we use in shaping who we are and what we are to become.

Marriages and friendships that last through the years are the result of the interplay of a hugely complex, mysterious, omnipotent force that shaped and continues to shape the universe and our own conscious or unconscious commitment to other beings. The "other beings" can be lovers, friends, children, grandchildren, dogs, cats. The point is that love is not sustained simply by whimsy or by chemistry. Rather, lasting loving relationships are the result of our own doing, our own commitment.

So, even though there are poems in here that don't directly deal in any way with romantic love, they do deal with love as it manifests itself in our lives, with loving relationships, with adoration and wonder of the world that was created by the eternal spirit of life and love, with affection for animals who become part of our loving families, with children and grandchildren whom we love and by whom we are loved. We all play parts in "making" loving homes and living loving lives.

The poems in this book could be characterized simply as vignettes of life, but I hope that the reader sees more in these poems, recognizes the myriad ways that love, the creative spirit that permeates our world and the universe beyond, and our own eagerness for and commitment to relationships that nourish and sustain us and frame our lives, weave together this world of wonder and mystery with which we have been gifted.

Ken Nye
December, 2006

"Welcome to Maine,
the Way Life Should Be"

THE CALL TO MORNING

I wish I could sleep late.
But I feel the sun
pulling me into the day
even when it's still well below the horizon
and the sky is only beginning to lighten.

Dawn is a magic time.

Occasionally deer linger in the orchard,
hoping to find just one more apple still clinging to
a lower branch.

The birds of early summer start their
love songs well before the sun rises,
lighting the morning air with a cacophony
of melodies and entreaties to
"come live with me and be my love."
(It's a wonder if any of these Caruso's of the tree tops
are ever denied by the ladies.)

Early morning dew has settled on everything,
giving even weeds the appearance of having
been misted by the florist's assistant
in order to freshen up the blossoms and bouquets.

Crows seem to think their role is to waken the world,
not with the lilting trills and trembling tongues
of cardinals and Baltimore orioles,
but with grating alarm clock cries
like the sounds that fill the air in an automotive repair shop.

But even the noise of the crows blends
with the symphony
sung by the song birds
and the breeze just beginning
to luff the leaves
that are still spreading themselves out
to inhale the sun.

My heart doesn't want to miss the day's beginning,
so my feet find the slippers on the floor in the dark,
the dogs sleepily stretch over to my kitchen chair
to nuzzle me a good morning,
and the day is begun
with melodies
and pollen perfume.

THE ERMINE

We had an ermine in the basement once,
but I didn't have any idea it was there.
I don't know what I would have done if
I had known.
But can you imagine that?
An ermine in the basement.

I went down four times a day
to feed the furnace pieces of wood
we had stacked in the fall.
When I stepped onto the dirt floor
at the bottom of the stairs
I inhaled,
not the musty stale air that most old
farmhouse basements produce,
but a fresh
potpourri of lumber yard
and wood shop.

A cozy, warm, sweet smelling world
with unlimited mice for meals,
that ermine must have thought he had died
and gone to heaven.

Actually, he knows better than I whether heaven
on earth can compare with the real thing,
because he did die.
That was the only time I saw him . . .
dead in the stacks of firewood.
As we methodically fed pieces of wood
to the furnace
through the winter,
we slowly peeled away the walls of his tomb.

One day, as I lifted a log from the pile,
there he was:
a beautiful purely white little weasel.
He must have died weeks before I found him;
he was as dry and stiff as cardboard.

But he was still beautiful.

That was the only ermine I have ever seen.

ICED OVER

I crossed a small brook yesterday
iced over like glass,
clear as a windowpane.

We are in mid-winter,
yet there was a little green tendril
of grass, blowing in the current,
like a tell-tail luffing on a sailboat shroud.

Clear water flowing over white sand
left by glaciers.
Rounded multi-colored pebbles,
nudged along by bubbles in the stream.

The sound of this little stream was muted,
like water flowing freely
in the basement after a pipe
has burst from the cold.
You had to pay attention to hear it.

But the melody from under the ice
reached me before I discovered its source.

There are times when I simply
wander in the woods,
following the whispers of music
that float in the silence of the wilderness,
from iced over stream beds to cedar waxwings in tree tops,
from whistling wind in dried field grass
to retreating waves spent on a windward lakeshore—
sights and sounds my soul remembers.

TUMBLEDOWN

Ask anyone who knows Maine's mountain trails
the best mountain for a single day climb
and they will tell you, "Tumbledown."

We park the car, load up
and, with bright morning light
sifting through the tender leaves of early summer,
start up the trail.

Ahead, we see through the vertical pattern of tree trunks
a huge boulder,
taller than most houses,
sitting where it landed
thousands of years ago
during some cataclysmic geologic shift.
As we scan the forest around us
we see smaller versions of this monolith
scattered indiscriminately among the trees,
giving the whole hillside the appearance
of a giant child's playroom before mother
has picked it up.

Passing the boulder
we begin the ascent,
in a short time laboring up
a steep trail,
moving from root to rock to root,
where thousands have stepped before us,
responding to the lure
of this mountain with an alpine lake at the top.

Eventually we reach the plateau,
halfway to the summit.
Fronting us are massive cliffs,
rising from this broad, impenetrable stream

of flowing granite outcroppings.
We follow the blue trail blazes
to the foot of the cliffs.
Like the hidden entrance to Shangri La,
the trail is screened by small trees growing
out of fissures in the rock.
We push through the brush and
follow a steep trail,
actually a dry stream bed, that
zigzags
back and forth across the face of the cliff.
Halfway up we stop and turn
to look out upon the Mahoosic Range,
one mountain silhouetted behind another,
mountain after mountain,
like a scene in my old Viewmaster.

The trail is so steep
we keep one hand out in front,
leaning against the vertical
rock path we
have yet to climb.

At the top of the trail
we are confronted by a pile of boulders,
stacked one upon the other,
jammed between the tops of the cliff faces
like a cork at the top of a giant rain gutter.
A blue marker
sends us under one of the big boulders
where iron rungs, hammered into the rocks,
lead up into the pile toward reflected daylight.

We peel off our packs,
and, mounting the iron rungs,
wiggle our way through the pile of boulders,
passing our packs along from hand to hand.

Emerging from the boulders
we are at the top of the cliffs.
To the left is the trail to the summit.
To the right the one to the pond.

The terrain and vegetation are alpine.
Wherever there is enough soil to sustain plant life
thick juniper stands, mountain blue berry bushes
and shriveled, stunted pines hold sway
among the
exposed rock outcroppings.

Unlike most mountain summits that slope down and away
in every direction,
up here there are more mountain summits
on the other side of another level rock plateau.
If we could fight our way through the dense brush,
we could hike to them and claim them as our own.
But we are anxious to see the pond,
so we turn to the right.

Hearing about this alpine lake at the top of the mountain
does not match the thrill
of cresting the granite cap and looking down upon
a pristine mountain pond with
crystal clear water
fed by springs
and an island in the middle.
We disappear into the brush surrounding the pond,
reappear in bathing suits
and gather at the pond's edge to test the temperature
of the water.
Surprisingly, it is not unbearably frigid,
so we gingerly tip toe deeper,
squealing like children as the cold water
envelopes us.

The strong swimmers immediately strike out
for the island, and in no time, we are on the rocks
at the island's edge.

We lie on the moss
that covers the island
and marvel at
this majestic panorama,
the sparkling water in front of us
rippling in the breeze,
the blue sky spotted with occasional clouds
that highlight silhouetted falcons
soaring high above the cliffs.

This mountain
and the scene before us
are almost dream-like.
But the chilled mountain water, like pinching ourselves,
tells us that it is real.

THE PRINCE OF THE FOREST

Even in the hushed silence
of this road through thick woods,
the bike's' rubber tires
are almost soundless.

Lost in thought,
I become aware of something up ahead
motionless in the middle of the road.

Getting a little closer, I see,
standing stock still, staring at me,
a magnificent male coyote.

Putting myself in his position,
I can imagine he's having trouble
coming up with an explanation for me,
this object silently moving toward him
without any apparent gait or lumber,
never varying the direction in which it moves
but inexorably coming closer.

When I get within fifty yards
I stop.
Both feet on the ground now,
straddling the bike,
I stand and stare at him,
just as he stands and
stares at me.

Then he spins and trots into the woods,
never looking back.

The majesty of this animal
was striking.
His lush multi-colored coat
fit him like a tailored robe.
And his demeanor spoke of
responsibilities and
decisions to be made.

I was but a trifle and easily dismissed.

THE CLAM FESTIVAL

Sitting in the back of our church booth
on Main Street,
resting my back after standing at the grille,
I'm in a huge nest.

Behind me is our church
in which I replenish spirit
and resolve.
It is the visible reason why we are selling
crab cakes and scallop rolls.

Around me are people I love.
My ten year-old granddaughter
is working the cash box,
calculating for a customer the cost of
three crab cakes,
two scallop rolls,
two tuna rolls,
four fruit drinks,
three spring waters,
three strawberry cheesecakes
and three peach shortcakes.
(She does this all day long and always gets it right!)
Scurrying to fill orders are my daughter and my wife.

Sitting in lawn chairs out on the curb are
my wife's 85 year-old mother
and her 90 year-old (boy) friend,
delighting in the parade.
(This parade is long.
It's like one of those freight trains at a railroad crossing that goes on forever.)
Somewhere in the parade
on a flat-bed truck
with other residents of her assisted living facility
is my 86 year-old mother,

who is today Dopey
in a Snow White tableau.
As her float finally rolls by,
I rush out with my camera
to catch "Grandma" with pixie ears,
throwing candy to kids,
waving and smiling and having a grand time.
(Later she was exhausted but exhilarated.)

Once the parade is over, business picks up,
and so does the foot traffic in front of our booth.
Periodically, I recognize past students of mine
heading to the carnival.
If they recognize me here at the grille,
they shout greetings,
while older students of mine,
heading the other way
with their sleepy little ones
clutching cones of partially eaten cotton candy,
say hi,
or, if sleep has already come to the treasures
in their arms,
whisper a greeting.

The lowly clam that lives buried in the mud of our
tidal estuaries
has never exhibited qualities of character
that would normally warrant making it the focus of a community endeavor
such as this.
But this event has to have a name.
And clams taste good when they are cooked.
So we call it the "Clam Festival."
But let's face it.
This isn't a celebration of clams.
I don't see a single clam
all weekend long.

But I see people who make up the fabric of my life.
This is a celebration of community,
church,
family,
friends,
summer.

This is the Clam Festival.

HYMNS OF JOY

I heard a whippoorwill last night
sing his wonder of the world.
The forest hushed,
caught in the spell
conjured by the whippoorwill.

At dawn his song could not be heard,
but in its place two cardinals sang
of love and light and nested grace.
And those who dared not hum last night
in deference to the whippoorwill
trilled and purred and sang their songs
in contrapuntal repartee.

I felt the joy heard in these hymns,
sung by forest denizens
who speak a language that echoes life
and moves my heart to sing.

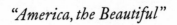

"America, the Beautiful"

ZION

I saw God today.

Emerging from the darkness of a
mountain tunnel,
I am stunned by giant pillars of red stone,
monolithic,
mountainous,
majestic.

I see swirls of multi-colored rock, once mud and sediment,
flung from one end of the canyon
to the other, a huge clay platter
thrown on
God's potter's wheel;
massive mountain slopes crisscross etched,
like graph paper;
giant arches, displaying
the unfathomable creative powers of wind
and rain
and time,
God's tools in the creation
of glory.

I heard God today.

Standing in the cool mist floating over us
from the stream of water falling into
the Emerald Pools,
I hear in the silence
only the staccato splashes
of the water not vaporized
by the breeze before it hits the canyon floor
and trickles into the still green saucers of sandstone.
The music of that mountain stream
speaks a language without words,
understood in our hearts.

I felt God today.

Sitting on a rock with my feet
dangling in the light brown water of
the Virgin River,
I sense the presence of a spirit of life
and creation,
an unbounded force not seen,
not heard as an entity in itself,
so grand in imagination and
generous in the conception and creation of
this world of unimagined beauty
that the mortal viewer can only overflow,
like a river,
with wonder.

Zion Canyon,
valley of peace and solitude,
cathedral of the living God
sculpting beauty
beyond our comprehension.

Written upon returning from a trip to Zion National Park, Utah.

THE NIOBRARA

We scattered Aunt Esther
into the Niobrara River this summer.
She was the last of my father's generation.
Raised in the sand hills of northern Nebraska,
my father and his four older siblings
always spoke lovingly of
their home territory.
And no wonder.
This is a pristine place
that few Americans know.

Standing on a bluff overlooking
the confluence of the Niobrara and Missouri rivers,
we could be in another century.
Lewis and Clark stood on this very promontory
and looked west, wondering,
(as they probably did at every turn in the river),
what they would find around the corner.
And at the same time they must have
marveled at this scene before them.

The Niobrara, in full flood from early summer rains,
is muddy and energetic as it swirls into the Missouri.
We can tell by the number of green shrubs and bushes
engulfed by the brown water that the river doesn't usually
carry this much water.
By mid-summer it will be a narrow riffle
down the middle of the sandy river bed.

The Missouri seems indifferent to the infusion
of the muddy Niobrara-Nebraska water
loaded with sand
and silt.

The brown water of the Niobrara is quickly
lost in the clearer, bluer water of the bigger river.

Standing on a sand bar in the middle of the river
is a bald eagle
waiting for an unsuspecting cat fish
to wander into the shallows.

A few hundred yards upriver from the eagle
is a flock of white pelicans,
standing in the sand and mud,
seemingly passing the time doing nothing.
Then, as if responding to a spoken command,
they run across the sand
and shallow water,
pumping their wings in unison
as they rise into the western sky
and burgeoning sunset.

Standing on this bluff overlooking the rivers,
we see no sign of man.
The hills of South Dakota on the other side
of the Missouri are covered with tall
prairie grass that bends in waves
as the constant breeze throws out
occasional gusts.

Over our heads soars a turkey vulture,
riding the thermal columns of warm air
rising up off the bluff.
As it passes between the sun and us
we can see the glow of sunlight through its
tail feathers.

Absorbed in the vulture and the view
of the rivers as we look north and east,

we don't see the mother turkey
and her seven little ones behind us in the grass
until, as our heads turn west to follow the pelicans,
the glare of the setting sun
forces us to lower our gaze.

Sensing they are now under observation,
the little turkeys disappear
and we wonder
how the mother got them
to scatter to hiding places so fast.
Pulling binoculars from my bag
and focusing on the mother hen,
I briefly glimpse a tiny turkey leg
under her fanned tail feathers.
I follow her with my glasses as they escape into the high grass,
and for just a few seconds
I see all seven of the little ones,
huddled under Mother's tail feathers
as she trundles along.
I can almost hear them complaining
about Mom walking too fast for them to keep up
and Mom admonishing them to hush up and stay under her tail.

As we drive down from the bluff at dusk,
deer are barely discernible in the deep shadows of
the adjoining hills.

I envy Aunt Esther.
What a place in which to spend eternity.
She is back in the sand hills of her childhood,
forever a part of this hidden corner of the country
with its unchanged beauty and pristine innocence.
The eagles and pelicans, turkeys and vultures,
deer and ground squirrels
are the keepers of the Niobrara.
When I go there, I am simply a visitor.

WANDERING THE ROADS OF NORTHERN NEBRASKA

We wander the roads of northern Nebraska,
getting the feel of the land and people.

Though the people are gone, their abandoned farms
paint portraits with what they left behind:
cooking utensils scattered like seeds,
implements hanging on weathered walls,
everything dusted with dirt and decay.

On the edge of the yard
in a muddy wetland
are broken and tangled cottonwoods,
once giving shelter from wind and sun,
lining what used to be
a small rivulet
flowing for poultry and pigs.

Rusty barbed wire
encircles the small overgrown pasture
and is ignored by the birds
who come and go as they please.

And the pump,
handle up,
poised to pour,
stands like an altar boy at a Mass for someone
no one loved.

There is no hope in these decrepit things.

Collapsed roof and broken porch steps
speak of families searching for
more than the land could deliver.

And so they moved on,
leaving the past to voice their despair.

WORLD HISTORY

Somewhere on this earth
may be a spot of dirt
on which man has never trod
and history has never been written.

But it is not beneath my feet.
The dirt of this old New England farmstead
is made up of clay from the mud flats,
dung from cows that used to graze here in what are now forests,
sand transported in wagons from the beaches
to lighten the loam.

The woods are not virgin soil.
They are laced with walls made of
stones pulled from the fields
laid into beds with other stones,
measured for their compatibility through the ages,
once delineating where one farm ended
and another began.

And it is not beneath the feet of the Frenchman
or the fair skinned Celt,
nor the feet of the blond Norseman.

It is not on the ground of ancient empires,
where chariots enforced decrees
and on which slaves
crawled into servitude.

It is not beneath the feet of the descendents of the
biblical warriors whose battles are still
being waged.

It is not in the steamy jungles of the Punjab,
or the pavilions of granite that rise to the sky.

It is not in the rice paddies of China,
the water chestnut terraces of Malaysia,
the tranquil meditation gardens of Japan.

Nor is it in the Outback,
scoured for centuries by aborigines
who have lived off the wild since
before the New World.

Maybe somewhere,
perhaps covered by a mile thick
sheet of ice,
is a piece of the earth's surface
on which no man has ever stepped.

But on all the rest of the earth's surface
is written
the history of our planet,
our country,
our neighborhood
in the footprints beneath us,
stamped into the skin of the earth
to be read by those who care
where the world has been.

CHOOSING

I look up to admire the
clean classic lines
of our white clapboard New England church,
but its white finger pointing to the sky
is fuzzy with flaking paint,
and broken and missing ceiling slats in the bell tower
give it the appearance of a Halloween hideaway
for bats and broomsticks.

Our church was built by
self-taught engineers and shipwrights
using the bounty of the forests at hand
and the strength in their arms and backs.

We, here in the 21st century,
cherish this structure
with its arrow of adoration
pointing to salvation,
recognizing it ties us to the past
and our heritage as a nation
forged in search of religious freedom.

But we are caught between devotion
to our history as a nation and people,
represented in the walls and spire of our church,
and the cost of maintaining this sepulcher of freedom,
built in another time,
with costs computed in a different way.

The builders of this church lived next door
or down the road,
walked in its doors every Sunday,
replaced a beam here and a strut there,
never thinking that two hundred years

would see the bounty of the forests
measured out in invoices and sales slips per board foot,
the forests providing the sills and posts
and siding and shingles oceans away,
the work of the people who rebuild or replace
or shore up calculated in dollars per hour.

And so, while the world continues to starve –
too little food,
too little water,
too little concern for human life —
our small church community must decide between saving the tower
on top of our timeless temple
and providing food and water and milk
to children who have none.

The steeple points to the heavens,
away from the misery of a world in need.
Our gaze tends to follow, but
our feet remain on the ground
and our hearts are torn.

CROSSING AMERICA, July 4, 2005

Crossing America,
I see small nations within its cities,
neighborhoods of people
who dream of happiness in myriad languages, and
who love America no less
because they cannot yet use the magic tongue.

A tenth generation American,
with roots that can be traced to
Boston gentry
and pioneers,
I wait in line
for a hamburger and milkshake with people who come from
the other side of the world,
still learning how it is done in the land of dreams.

Crossing America,
I hear children pledge fealty to our flag
and hope that what sometimes is
an exercise in thoughtless ceremony
will produce adults with unshakeable commitment
to what that flag represents.

Crossing America,
I feel the never ceasing breeze that sweeps
the prairies of our good fortune,
hear the soft whistle of wind through the tall
grasses of the Dakotas,
see the hot brown exhaust of Nebraska-baked feed lots
blowing east to mingle with the smoke from
the stacks of Gary and Elizabeth.

Crossing America,
I mistake the mountains on the horizon
for storm clouds, and am struck dumb
by the massive Rocky Mountain wall of sandstone and shale,
once an ocean bottom,
that rises up like a monolithic Wall of China
from the flat, legend crusted plains
of Oklahoma, Colorado, Wyoming, Montana.

Crossing America,
I am light headed, not only from the thin air above the tree line
in the Saw Tooth, the Wind River, the Tetons,
but the beauty of the twisted mountain pines,
the shriveled Douglas fir that have been raised by
never ending winds on the heights of the Continental Divide.

Crossing America,
I hide from the desert heat of Utah and Nevada
in my air-conditioned car and
welcome the stops at mid-desert oases
of one-armed bandits and neon lights.

Crossing America,
I crest the peaks of the Cascades and the Sierra Nevada,
see reflections of the sun glinting off waves in the ocean
that bounds the western end of the land of freedom.

Crossing America,
I feel its pulse in cities and small hamlets,
am comforted by the warmth of its people,
lifted up by the common love of liberty
and the universal dream of peace.

Crossing America
I am in a car without a yellow ribbon
that says, "Support our troops."
How could I not?
They are my sons,
my daughters.
White, black, yellow, red,
they are my children.

As I travel across America,
l thank the god
who created such beauty,
who nurtured a nation born in defiance of tyranny
and dedicated to justice and equality.

And I marvel at my good fortune
to live in this time,
in this land,
with these people.

Friends and Family

APPRECIATING THE TABLEWARE

I took the morning off today
so I could stop in and see old friends,
actually sit down and get caught up.

One of my best friends from high school and I
have stayed in touch through the years.
Intervals between our meetings are getting shorter.
We seem to cherish these moments now,
not take them for granted any more.
He has prostate cancer;
I have Parkinson's.

As we get older,
my male friends and I
are more apt to hug when we say goodbye.
We start with a handshake,
but as soon as our hands meet,
we seem to realize
our friendship warrants
an embrace.

In that moment
we silently acknowledge
things never spoken:
that we are mortal and the clock is ticking;
that goodbyes at our age have a greater
chance of being final;
that friendships that have lasted
through the years are sterling, not plate.

There was a time when I didn't
pay much attention to the tableware.
Now I'm starting to see
the beauty in a pattern of silver,
the brilliance of freshly polished sterling,
the rich patina of age.

I should take the morning off more often.

PRELUDE TO GOODBYE
October, 2005

We began to say goodbye to Mom years ago,
even when she always knew who we were.
Yesterday she thought I was my brother,
and for a brief moment the conversation went awry.
I gave her little hints to straighten her out,
and she picked up on them,
steering the conversation back in the right direction.
She has learned to cover such mistakes.
Always a proud lady, she still refuses a walker or wheel chair,
shuffling along,
negotiating the world
on her own.

Grandchildren and great grandchildren
are general concepts to her now.
Her "family" has narrowed down
to her four children.
Birthday parties for family members
are occasions of general confusion.
She forgets whose birthday it is,
who all these people are,
why everyone has gathered.

She tells stories of the "old days,"
creations of her imagination and
dreams and fantasies.
The grandchildren and great grandchildren
look to us when Grandma begins to talk about
the alligator at her house in Florida
that came across the back lawn
and tried to climb up the sliding glass door.

They know Grandma never lived in Florida,
that, even though we are all
sitting at the same table
Grandma is somewhere else right now.
We wink back at them.
Waiting for me to pick her up,
she appears anxious and apprehensive,
like a little girl sitting outside the school office,
waiting for her mom to come get her.
She studies the other cars that arrive before mine,
trying to find a face she recognizes,
no longer sure why she is waiting for me in the first place.
"Now where are we going?"

But when the conversation turns to my health,
she is Mom again,
in her element, caring for her boy.
She questions me about what the doctor said,
encourages me to do exactly as he says,
wonders aloud why her son should develop
this problem.
"No one else in the family ever had it."

We say goodbye to Mom when we drop her off.
But we are aware that the conversation in the car
has been part of our goodbye,
that just spending time with her
is part of our goodbye,
that every "goodbye" is part of the prelude
to the final goodbye.

There are brief moments when the real "Mom"
is with us again,
and when that happens
we know how precious
those moments are.

A BEAUTIFUL YOUNG WOMAN

I saw a beautiful young woman today
whom I had not seen before.
But she was familiar to me.
Something about the smile touched a memory
of my little granddaughter and me sharing a joke.
But the smile on this beauty
is going to entrap some unsuspecting boy.
He won't have a chance.

I watched a beautiful young woman today
moving comfortably among friends,
confidant and poised,
a joy to watch.
Something about her manner reminded me
of my little granddaughter celebrating her birthday
with friends.

My eyes followed a beautiful young woman on a bicycle today,
riding down the road in front of our house.
Something about the grace and dignity of her movements
reminded me of my little granddaughter
getting the hang of the two wheeler,
not yet ready to stand up to pedal.
But this lithe rider with an athletic build
was in control of everything around her.

I could watch this beautiful young woman all day long.

FAMILY HISTORY

I think I was nine
when my dad
stopped giving me a kiss goodbye.
We shook hands after that.

I don't remember my father
telling me he loved me—
ever.
But I never doubted
that he did.
As a matter of fact, the absolute presence of my
father's love was a pillar of my growing up.
When I was in athletics, he never missed a game –
not a one.
On some afternoons,
he would be the only spectator in
our section of the bleachers.
When I hit the only triple I ever hit
in my baseball career,
he hollered, "Atta boy!"
when I was just breaking away from home plate.
(I can still hear him.)
I was running the bases for him.

When he was on what he thought was
his death bed,
he told me he was proud of me.
(We had to have the threat of death
to bring that out of him.)
That was shortly after his first heart attack.
(He died of the third.)
That was as close as we ever came to speaking
of love.

I learned how to be a man
from my dad.
Much of what I learned
has served me well,
given me direction,
bolstered my behavior
with rock solid principle.

But I have spent my life
trying to unlearn some of it, too.
It is amazing to me how difficult
it still is for me to tell my own kids
I love them.

I hope they know.

THE SHEPHERD

They came to us young and glowing,
a shepherd and his wife,
fresh threads
to be woven into the warp of this church,
he with a presence that belied his age,
she with a smile that rivaled sunshine.

Wielding his staff with care and compassion,
he has guided us from pasture to pasture,
mountainside to mountainside.
His voice carries the warmth of family,
the security of sanctuary,
the welcome of friendship.

When he speaks to the heavens,
he includes us all,
remembering our joys,
our fears,
our sorrows.

Shedding his shepherd's cloak,
he becomes a street clown,
a juggler,
a breather of fire.

On Christmas Eve he morphs into
a poor carnival castoff
who gives his only possession of worth
to celebrate the birth of a baby.

Ten years have passed.
Suspenders now are glimpsed beneath the shepherd's cloak;
his beard mirrors his age and wisdom.
And we, his flock, are comforted by his care,

grateful for his affection,
challenged by his gentle suggestions
of ways to
change the world.

In gratitude we celebrate
these ten years together,
we and this shepherd of our hearts,
proud that the pattern in the fabric of this church
has grown brighter still and
sings with the spirit of life.

*Written in celebration of the tenth anniversary
of the ministry of Erik Wikstrom,
First Universalist Church,
Yarmouth, Maine
September 11, 2005*

THE QUEEN OF HEARTS

Our lives are measured
by little things.

We have a doll in our family,
a gift to our daughter
when she was just
learning to talk.
When she opened the wrapped package
that Christmas forty years ago,
her face melted in emotion,
and she raised the doll to her heart,
as if she were giving it life
by her embrace.

When asked the baby's name
she responded,
"Sandy."
(Straight from a little girl's imagination.)
Sandy became part of our family.
The two were inseparable.
When Sandy was misplaced,
there was no sleeping in our house,
no television diversion from the crisis.
A child was missing.

Even into her teen years,
my daughter gave Sandy
the center spot on her pillow.

Eventually a granddaughter entered our lives.
The doll,
given a new cloth body by Gram,
was wrapped up at Christmas
and presented to our new little one who,

like her mother,
lifted the adored child to her heart
and made her her own.
The reborn doll was christened "Baby Santa Claus."
(A curious amalgamation.)

My granddaughter, now thirteen,
has enthroned Baby Santa Claus on her bed
with a court of
stuffed animals paying homage
at her feet.
She is the matriarch now,
a virgin queen of little girls' hearts.

There is magic in this little doll.
I suspect that down the road,
if a great granddaughter is gifted to us,
we will once again watch in wonder as
Baby Santa Claus, nee Sandy,
is unwrapped for the third time
and lifted into another little girl's heart.

I hope I get to see it.

BIG BROTHER

I lie awake, listening for him.
But I don't hear anything except my brother breathing
in his sleep, as though this was just any old night.
(He sounds like the dog having a nightmare.)
I can hear Dad snoring down the hall.
What is wrong with these people?
Why aren't they awake?

What am I going to do if I hear him?

I'm not going down there by myself.

I wonder what time it is.

"Wake up! Wake up!" my brother is whispering,
but it sounds like shouting to me.
Why should I wake up?
What's going on?
"Come on. Let's go," he whisper shouts,
not waiting to see if I'm following.
Wait a minute! Is he here?
I'm not going down there if he's here.
"He's not here now, idiot. It's almost five o'clock.
Come on. Let's go!"

As we tip toe down the stairs, we can see
the glow from the lights on the tree
even before we get to the landing.
I'm not so sure about this.
Man, if he's here, I'm going back to bed fast!
"Oh, shut up, idiot. He left a long time ago."

He stops on the landing and peeks around the corner.
Makes me feel better.

He doesn't want to walk in on him either,
(even though he won't admit it).

The living room dimly glows,
lit only by the lights on the tree.
There are two distinct piles of stuff,
their cellophane wrappers glittering in the rainbow of lights.

Hey! The cocoa's gone! So is the cookie!
My gosh, he left a whisker again.
He really was here!

"Idiot!"

WHAT'S IN A NAME?

Jennifer Robin is a person in herself,
but she never knew the Robin
who shares her name.
Those of us who did might think
the gift of the name included
a piece of the heart.

I remember Robin, when she was ten.
(That's how old Jennifer is now.)
She was a sparkplug of energy,
a ham on the family stage,
an athlete wary of the worry of defeat,
but not willing to be in the shadow of
a big sister whom she adored.
I can see Robin in my Jennifer Robin.

As Jennifer Robin grows into a woman,
she carries more than the same name.
She carries pieces of our hearts that we
gave to Robin when she left us.

My father's name was given to me,
and his and my name was given to my son.
We, like Jennifer Robin,
have an extra responsibility
as we grow through life
that some inheritors of other's names
may not like:
We create shadows that are a tiny bit larger
than the persons we are.

But the mystery of this gift of a name
is that the child who never knew the person
whose name she shares,
reflects the soul of her namesake.

And that is a joy to those who loved one
and now love the other.

What's in Jennifer Robin's name?
Right now it's a little ten year old girl
with a heart and soul of her own,
nurtured by another soul called Robin.

PRAYER FOR A SOLDIER

Unknowable architect of this world of wonder,
bring our soldier safely home
after his duty is done.

Make his time in uniform a sacred memory
of service to peace,
of sacrifice for others,
of love of country and devotion to family.

Help him to understand
the power he now wields
and that glows from his uniform,
that he is not a conqueror
or avenging angel,
that the vanquished people around him
now look to him for help
as they strive to piece their world back together.

Lead him to cherish his brothers in arms
and hold fast to
the bonds of friendship,
forged in the nightmare of battle,
that will,
through the years,
be a source of comfort and support.

Make his time in uniform a lesson in human hearts:
Help him to endure the selfish soldier who
cares more for himself
than his companions and those he is to protect,
to offer friendship to the lonely soldier
longing for home
and a friendly face,
to recognize the voice of a leader who doesn't care,

and to avoid the leader
who seeks the status of myth.

Keep him mindful of the heritage of America,
of our nation's rock solid belief
in freedom, equality and compassion for others.
Help him to be a missionary of the American dream.

And, spirit of life and love,
wonderful, mysterious, magical maker of the universe,
enfold our soldier in your loving arms
until he returns to ours.

THE ANGEL OF GUATEMALA CITY

The bell tolls today.
The world is a bit less wonderful,
the future a little less bright.

An angel has gone home.

A beautiful young blonde woman,
late twenties,
summering in Guatemala City
so she could learn to speak the language,
about to leave for home.
"Before you go, I want you to see something."

Guatemala City Dump,
steam rising from piles of garbage,
dogs and vultures scavenging,
and men and women and children,
bent over, sifting through the debris,
searching for food,
tin,
aluminum —
any thing that can be eaten,
anything that can be sold.

"Who are these people?" she asks.

"They live here."

"In Guatemala City?"

"In the dump."

"Where are there their homes?"

"Look carefully."

She goes home,
sells her car,
sells her computer,
sells everything that she can do without
and returns to this city
and to the people who live in the dump.

Because she came back,
because she said to the world,
"This is not acceptable.
I will not let these children go hungry.
I will not let these children remain illiterate,
to live and die in this dump,"
600 children go to school in uniforms,
with full stomachs
and arms full of books,
and hearts brimming with hope.

But the bell tolls today.
The angel has gone home.

And there is grief unimaginable.

Written in the hour of the memorial service for
Hanley Denning, age 36, founder of Safe Passage,
Guatemala City, Guatemala

IN THE MIDDLE OF THE NIGHT

Having explained that
wild animals come out at night,
I suggest
we take flashlights
up to the cliff and wait until deep darkness sets in when
we can see all kinds of things.

They aren't enthused about this venture,
but, trusting their dad knows
what he's talking about,
they silently put on their jackets,
turn on the flashlights,
and we three head up into the woods
toward the cliff.

It is dusk as we walk up the Old County Road,
and when we get to the deepest sections of the forest
it's almost pitch black.
But there is just enough light
filtering through the overhead canopy
to enable us to see where we are going and,
having hiked up to the cliff
so many times before,
we don't have any trouble
getting to the overlook.

We all sit down on the granite ledge
and gaze out on our valley as it
dims into darkness.
They are sitting close to me,
one on each side.
Nobody says anything for a while.

Finally, one of them asks, "Where are the animals?"
I tell them we just have to sit quietly
and eventually we'll hear something rustling
in the grass
or bushes, and when we do
we'll turn on our flashlights
and see what it is.

They don't want to see what it is.
I ask, "What do you mean?"
They respond in unison, "This is scary."
I try to reassure them
if we shine the lights
on an animal,
it will be more frightened of us
than we are of it.

"I want to go home."
"Me too."

I plead that we came all the way up here to see animals.
Let's not give up so easily.

"I want to go home."
"Me too."

So we begin the climb down.
Coming up they had enough light to still feel
secure on their own.
But now they both want the reassurance of my hand.
No, they don't want to hold each other's hands;
they want to hold my hand.
That means I can't hold a flashlight.
They forget
if they are holding the flashlights
they have to shine them in the direction in which
we want to go.
"I can't see where we're going, guys.

You've got to shine the lights on the path."

"I'm scared."
"Me too."

It takes us three times as long to get home
as it did to get up to the cliff.
Halfway home they become convinced we are lost.
My adamant reassurance we are on the trail
to the house
does not convince them.

Whimpering starts.

I am not having a good time.

We finally can see the lights of the house.
The whimpering stops.

Once inside they sullenly take off their jackets.
Mom asks what did we see?
We all respond, "Nothing."

But I learn that unless little children
are used to being in the middle of the woods
in the middle of the night,
the only thing that comes out at night
are little kid's fears of the woods
in the middle of the night.

We never try this again.

EVERYDAY COURAGE
March, 2007

My mother is 89.
She has Alzheimer's.

She lives in an assisted living
retirement lodge.
Her friend is Eleanor.
Mom can't remember Eleanor's name,
but she knows that woman
is her friend.

There are other people
at the lodge.
All need assistance of one kind
or another.
They stick together.

After breakfast, assisted by an arm of another
or a wheeled walker,
they go out and sit on the front porch
and watch the cars go by.
They don't talk much.

At noon they gather outside the dining room
and wait for the lunch bell.
When it rings, they roll in
behind their walkers,
find their tables,
sit and wait
for the help to park their walkers
in the "garage,"
(the big closet next to the dining room).

After lunch they assemble in the living room
and wait for the van to come around to the front.
Then they all pull themselves up onto their feet
and shuffle out to the portecochere
where the staff
take their walkers
and lift them up into the van.

They love the van ride.
The driver says he goes
to the same places every day
and his passengers are just as thrilled
seeing the sights the tenth time
as they were the
first.
Every trip is to someplace new.

When we told Mom
in the morning
we were coming up
in the evening
to take her out to dinner,
she remembered only
that she was going out.
So she put on her best outfit
and then went downstairs to wait all day
(until the staff distracted her).
We have learned not to tell her we are coming.
And she is always surprised and thrilled.

As she struggles to get into
or out of the car,
she makes jokes about herself.
She can't make much sense
of most of the conversation at
our Christmas dinner.

She gets frustrated that she can't remember which
grandchildren belong to which of her children.
(Some grandchildren she no longer remembers at all.)
She wishes she could still drive,
but she knows she couldn't
find her way
home.

She still smiles a great smile when she sees us.

She marvels at the shape of clouds
with childlike delight.
Her eyes water up when we see a western sky
melt into a sunset masterpiece or
when we turn down a road lined with
autumn colors.

She still exclaims in wonder when we
stroll through the rose garden and she smells
the different fragrances of orange and peach
and scarlet, and white, and soft yellow cream.
She still looks to each day to accomplish something,
rises up every morning and gets the day underway.

She never stops seeing beauty in the world.
And she never stops loving us
and trusting us to take care of her.

She knows she is in a waiting place.
And she knows what she is waiting for.

My mother sings a song of courage every day.
I hope I can sing the same song
when my turn comes.

Furry Family Members Who Throw-Up on the Rug

WHAT IS IT ABOUT A DOG?

What is it about a dog,
these almost-half-human animals
who choose us over
their own kind?
Is it the look in the eyes?
The silent pledge of loyalty
and holy commitment?

Is it the shy but determined approach toward
the hand of a stranger, held out for inspection and approval,
the obvious desire to please?
Is it the joyful ecstacy that pours from
the face,
the happy canine grin,
the wild exuberance of a tail out of control
when the master returns or
the leash is pulled from the closet?

Was there ever a creature more forgiving,
willing to accept responsibility
for whatever is wrong in your life
that prompted that unfair
reproof and harsh word of rejection?

Does anyone else read your body language
as accurately?
Are the heavy thoughts in your head
as apparent to anyone else
as they are to your dog,
who always knows what you are feeling
and who always offers support
with a nudge of the arm
or a wet love swipe with the tongue?

What do you suppose happened in God's world
that gave him the idea to create a dog?

Loyal friend, loving companion,
ever present attendant who offers
love without boundaries,
devotion without reason.

A dog is a gift.

"WHERE HAVE THEY BEEN KEEPING THIS STUFF CALLED 'TABLE SCRAPS'?"

The vet called with the biopsy report.
It's the bad kind of cancer.
She said chemo could control it for a while,
could give him another year or so.
But it's going to cost money.

Calling him a "family pet"
seems to put him into the same category
as a favorite easy chair, something you grow
comfortable with but when it's too old
and beat up to keep around
you drop it off at the Salvation Army
and go and get another one.

But the comfortable easy chair
doesn't love you unconditionally like
this old warrior who protects us from squirrels
and low flying planes,
who monitors our moods like a weather man and
moves in with a love swipe of his raspy tongue
when he senses somebody is down.

If there is anything good to be said about all of this,
it is that he doesn't have any idea what's going on.
All he knows is that he's feeling good again.
He's not worrying about the cancer coming back
or about getting sick from the chemo.
He'll just take one day at a time,
relish the opportunities each day gives him
to eat great food,
("Where have they been keeping this stuff called
'table scraps'?")

ride in the back seat,
stick his head out the window
and let the wind blow his cheeks out.
It's a great life and there are no worries about the future.
There is still a smile on his face.

We'll go with the chemo therapy,
give him as much time as we are allowed.
We're probably going to spoil him rotten.

I'll call the vet.

LET'S GO FOR A RIDE

I get the same response that I've always gotten:
a look of excitement and joy,
immediate effort to rise and head for the car.
But rising is now a major project,
and jumping up into the
back seat is not possible.
So I lift him up, moving mechanically,
trying to drive my grief and dread down into my gut.

How many times have I said, "Let's go for a ride"?
The sunroof was for him so he could stand
on the center console and poke his huge head up
through the roof and survey the passing world
like a tank commander.
I got a kick out of people smiling and pointing
when they saw him.
No smile for him, though.
Piloting this tank is serious business.

But no more tank commander trips, now.
Legs are too wobbly.

He just lazes on the back seat,
enjoying being with me.
I talk to him and get the usual unspoken,
"I don't have any idea what you are talking about,
but I love you anyway" look.

White hair around the face now,
eyes glazed with age.
Even though he can barely see,
he'll go wherever I go.
That's been his life purpose.

My hands shake on the wheel
as I contemplate our farewell.

Only a little while back he was an armful of puppyness,
for years a constant companion and playmate,
always striving to do what I wanted him to do.
Snuggling down on my feet under the desk,
he wanted to be close.

So I owe him this last trip,
when he is still a dignified presence
in the backseat.
We'll park the car, I'll put the leash on him
and help him down.
And, when he recognizes where we are,
he'll begin to shake like he always does.
But, like a trooper, he'll go wherever I go.

I will miss him so.

REMINDERS OF A DOG NOW GONE

We no longer have dog-hair tumbleweeds
blowing along the surface of the hardwood floors or
lurking in corners and crevasses of wall and baseboard.
But occasionally, cleaning an out-of-the-way closet,
I come across another dainty phantom-like wisp
of golden retriever underdown that reminds me of him.

Waxing the bathroom floor,
I see the chewed edges of the baseboard
where he experimented with wood trim
as a way to pass the time until we got home.

Out in the garage, looking for the plumber's snake
with which to probe the septic line,
I confront at eye level his choke-chain collar
with the license tag
hanging from a nail in one of the ceiling joists.
It seems to be out of place, hanging from a nail.
It belongs around his neck.

I wonder what the point is now of a car with a sunroof.
No big golden retriever to stand on the center console
and make the world smile.

Rather than making me sad, though,
these unexpected encounters with a dog now gone
warm my mood,
soften any edges clinging to thoughts and attitudes
of the moment,
much in the same way he leveled my emotions
and put a smile on living.

He is still here and there,
still a presence in my heart.

GOLDEN RETRIEVER RESCUE

Our golden retriever died a few weeks ago.
He was eleven.
Our house was empty and my heart was hollow,
but I figured I'd wait until summer to get a puppy.

One empty day followed another.
There was no dog at my feet at the breakfast table,
no thumping tail drumming a welcome against the side of the car
as I drove into the garage,
no pestering wet nose flipping my arm
off the computer keyboard to
remind me it's dinner time.

The world probably thought I was the same person,
but my wife knew something was missing.
She called the local Golden Retriever Rescue network;
found two golden retriever/Lab "mixed breeds"
waiting for a home.
Raised together and
abandoned together,
the shelter wanted them to go out together.
We went up to "see if you like them."

My days now start with a group hug and
a lovingly administered face wash,
a new morning ritual that makes me wonder
who rescued whom.

I NEVER MET A PUPPY I DIDN'T LIKE

I can always tell when a dog has been trained
and when it hasn't.
I prefer the trained ones,
but even the wild ones can be fun
if they still love people.

Once in a while, though, I see a dog
straining at his chain,
lips curled as he hurls oaths of hatred at me,
dragging his dog house toward me in an effort
to latch on to my leg or tear my face.
I think to myself,
"Why in the world would anyone want a dog like that,"
one who apparently hates people and would maul them
if he could?

And then I wonder if that dog came out of the litter box
as an eight-week-old puppy,
angry and full of fury,
not longing to kiss the master's nose
but rather to set his little teeth into the master's cheek jowls.

When does a dog turn bad?

Can there be such a thing as a "vicious puppy"?

I have never seen one.
And I have spent time with myriad puppies.

When I was a boy
I worked at a private kennel
owned by millionaires,
a hunting family who raised cocker and English spaniels
for companionship and field work.

I cleaned out pens,
took young adult dogs for walks in the fields,
getting them used to leashes,
preparing them for full-time training on leash and off.

The highlight of my day was my half-hour lunch break,
when, after inhaling a tuna fish sandwich,
I stepped into the puppy pen,
sat down with my back against the wall,
and fifteen to thirty puppies, squealing in delight,
swarmed over to me, onto my lap, climbing my chest,
trying to give me kisses.
It was always a joy-filled thirty minute love fest.

I never saw a bad puppy,
never experienced a puppy bite offered as anything other
than a love bite.

Where, then, do bad dogs come from?

THE PROMISE

I lie back in the chair
and place the puppy
that smells of warm milk
on my chest.
She crawls up under my chin
and tries to suckle.
Getting no results,
she snuggles down to sleep
on my neck,
breathing contentment into my ear,
whispering her promise of life-long devotion.

THE TIGER

I watch, fascinated, as the cat
moves as smoothly as a snake,
crouching low to the ground,
placing her paws soundlessly into the dead grass,
ears turned directly ahead,
eyes steady and locked onto her prey
(which I can't see but do not doubt is there).
Then she freezes, her long tail
twitching from side to side.
Concentrating her entire being on the object
in front of her, she begins to tremble as she prepares to strike.
Then, like an arrow shot from a crossbow,
she springs and pounces.
Holding down the field mouse that squirms in terror,
she engulfs it with her mouth, and begins to carry it
back toward the house.
I can see that it's still alive.

When she reaches the foot of the steps
she gently places the mouse on the ground
and releases it.
The mouse scrambles away, and the cat
lopes along beside it for a few feet
and then pounces on it again,
lifts it up in her mouth and brings it back
to the foot of the steps
where she releases it again.

Again the mouse takes off in terror,
and again she playfully skips along
after it and then smothers it with her paws,
taking it up in her mouth and
bringing it back to the steps.

I wonder how long this is going to go on.
It grates against my civilized upbringing.
I begin to think that I should save the mouse.
My heart, raised on Gus Gus
and the mouse colony who outfitted Cinderella,
is championing the field mouse
whose life has become a plaything
to the cat.

I start to attribute an evil disposition
to this cat
who has given birth to a litter of kittens on my
daughter's bed
while she slept.
I am shocked and dismayed to see
this member of our family acting
like a wild animal, enjoying the
slow kill of the mouse.

And then it dawns on me:
this family member is,
before anything else,
not a sweet little cuddly ball of fur,
but an animal who by nature
hunts smaller animals and kills them—
and eats them, leaving just the liver
on the back attic stairs
so we will be impressed.

I decide to let the cat be a cat,
let the field mouse suffer,
and let the natural order of things
play itself out at the bottom of our steps.

But I stop watching
and leave,
still rooting for Gus Gus.

Ponderings

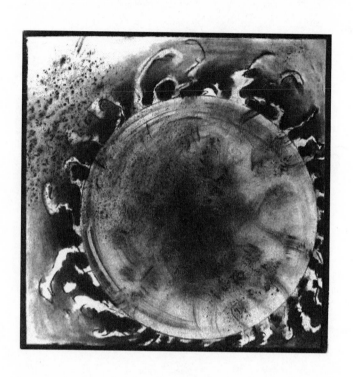

THE FIRST DAWN

The universe still reverberates with the concussive
blast of the beginning,
traveling at the speed of light
to the furthest edges of eternity.
It's possible there are places in the universe
so far away they
are only now receiving light from the explosion.

But our world was blasted into orbit around our sun
in that incomprehensible explosion of creation
and, with only minor variations in its departure and arrival times
over the eons,
the sun has delivered dawn every day since.

Was there darkness on the
only hours-old horizon,
and then, for the first time,
a lightening in the east?
An orange, reddish, pastel in the sky
presaging sunshine?

As the contours of the land became discernible
and the world was revealed,
were there faint shadows
that became distinct, as the sun
rose from behind the horizon
and set that first day in motion?

BEAUTIFUL AND NOT

Let us speak of what is beautiful.

I suspect somewhere in the human organism,
maybe in a gene or two,
is the formula that tells us something is
beautiful.

We seem to agree that the carcass of a skunk,
spread thin by tires on the white line of a road
is not a beautiful thing.
And a watermelon sky at sunset
with silver highlights at clouds' edges
and a gold nugget hovering on the horizon is.

There are always sights and sounds
that do not fit the formula
and receive mixed reviews.
And there are always people
who see beauty where most do not,
or find no beauty where most do.

(But let's attribute that to mutation.)

GARDEN GLOVES

Why would someone wear gloves to work
in the garden?
I can see wearing gloves
while you manhandle rocks
out of the ground,
try to remove the roots of an overgrown yew tree
or haul downed limbs to a fire.
But not when you're
down on your hands and knees
working the soil,
planting a border or the fixings
for a summer salad.

Yes, you get dirt under your fingernails,
you may inadvertently grab a slug
as you scoop out a hole in which to
place a seedling.

But wearing gloves to work in the garden
is like wearing clothes
while making love.
With gloves on,
you can't feel the warmth of the soil,
the different textures of dirt.
You won't feel the contours of the garden bed change,
lose their cold resisting compactness
as you work the humus in,
become
soft
and compliant.

You won't experience what a gardener
is seeking –
losing oneself in the
timeless ritual of
planting seed,
promoting life,
anticipating beauty,
going to the earth itself
for connection,
renewal,
and unspoken purpose.

THE GIRL IN THE PARIS SUBWAY

In Middle Eastern dress,
head covered by a thin white burqa,
a 16 or 17 year-old girl
sits on the stairs leading down to the subway,
one hand extended,
palm up.
She stares at the floor,
face vacant,
lost,
empty of hope,
beyond despair.

The last in a group of six travelers
late on their way out of Paris,
I stop,
struck by this girl who does not belong here,
reach into my pocket and
gather the loose change
of unused Euros and
drop them into her hand.

I want to ask her name,
why she is here,
what I can do to help.

But I am late,
bringing up the rear.
I cannot speak her language,
nor she mine.

So I turn up the stairs and
resume my flight to the waiting train.

Growing Old Together

GROWING OLD TOGETHER
Another poem for Ann

You come out to me in the kitchen
in your pajamas,
give me a hug and a kiss
and say, "Happy Anniversary."
Aware that the only thing between me and your skin
is one thin layer of cotton,
I begin to consider ways of coaxing you back into the bedroom.
As you get out a cereal bowl and look for the Raisin Bran
I take advantage of the cozy confines of our kitchen area
that require you to brush past me as you move from
cupboard to refrigerator to sink,
and gently tug at your pajama top
as you pass by me,
making what I
and my testosterone
feel certain are self-explanatory
suggestions.
You stop and give me a quick kiss,
murmuring in my ear, "Later."

Ever the pragmatist in our 44 year marriage,
and always the final decision-maker
on whether or not we go to bed to do anything
other than read or sleep,
your eye is on the clock.
The world isn't going to stop
to give us the time for the celebration
of this day that I have in mind,
so the celebration will have to wait.

As you prepare for the day ahead,
you whistle to yourself through your teeth,
producing a sound more like melodic hissing
than true whistling,
But it is a sound I have come to cherish.

To say that I've "grown accustomed to your face"
does not accurately state my condition.
Henry Higgins was only in the early stage
of his relationship with Liza
when he began to realize how integral to his life
her mannerisms and behaviors
had become.

Your whistle,
the way you curl your toes when you're barefoot,
your total absorption when involved in a project
that has captured your enthusiasm and creativity,
the way you move across a room,
and myriad other things about you
have become pillars
of the framework with which
I have come to understand the world.

Looking into the years ahead
with their diminishing number
of mornings like this one
with you,
I cannot dismiss the lurking feeling of foreboding
that trembles through me.

But, when those glimpses of the future
slip past my defenses,
my mind turns to you in the present,
and the things about you
imbedded in my heart
that are anchors of stability and security
as we face together the challenge of growing old.

I am a lucky man that I have you.

(And I can't wait until we get to "later.")

MAKING LOVE

As years go by and passions cool,
we make love in places that
young lovers only dream about.

We make love at the kitchen table,
a Scrabble board the mattress
and hints to help the other
our passionate kisses.

We make love in the car,
thrilling to beautiful scenery
or the sighting of a rarely seen wild animal.

We make love in front of the fireplace,
watching a game show and
sharing our latest craft creations.

We make love on the middle school hockey field,
proudly watching our granddaughter
dribble the ball down the field
with half the opposing team
in hot pursuit.

We make love in the bathroom,
where I marvel at the beauty of my
companion and friend of so many years
and tell her as she lathers all over
that she is the prettiest girl I know.

We make love in bed with our pajamas on,
she curled up against me, spoon on spoon,
feeling each other's warmth and whispering before
falling into sleep, "I love you."

We are so shamelessly promiscuous,
we make love in church, for god's sake,
sharing the hymnal hand on hand,
touching during prayers to say to the other
without words or looks,
"You are the rock of my happiness."

Wonderfully, heavy breathing is still in our repertoire.

But the bond between us that will challenge even death
is the love made here and there,
time and time again,
side by side.

WASN'T THAT YOU?

After you turned out the light tonight
you reached over and latched on to my arm.
But wasn't that you who tenderly held my arm
as you sat next to me
on the way to Jones' Beach after graduation?
(My arm was browner then,
more muscular.)

Looking up from the floured counter top
and the biscuit batter, you stood on your tip toes
and gave me a kiss.
But wasn't that you who huddled with me
in long embraces
out behind the refrigerator
by the back door,
waiting for your mother to flash the lights?
(We were seventeen.)

Changing the school photos of our granddaughters
to mark the passing of another year,
you mused, "They're starting to look like young women.
Aren't they beautiful?"
But wasn't that you who changed the pictures
of our three year old son,
telling me
how hard it was to get him to sit quietly
for the photographer this time?

Wasn't that you?

TEARING DOWN THE OLD CAMP

I am standing on the roof of the old camp,
Skilsaw in hand,
in the process of dismantling this place
I helped to build.

When I was six,
my brother and I hauled the wood
I am now ripping through with my saw
up the path from the parking area
at the end of the road.

Carrying two fourteen foot boards a hundred yards
down a root and rock strewn path
through the deep woods of a Maine hillside
was no easy trip for a six year old.
That first summer my mom and dad and brother and I
put up the first room of what eventually evolved into
our summer palace.

I contributed in more significant ways
in the building of the "master bedroom"
and the "boys' sleeping porch"
and the front deck,
additions through the years.
I grew along with the camp.

The camp is now almost sixty years old.
Parts of it have already been amputated.
What's left is not worth restoring.

My son is working next to me.
He knows only what I have told him
about how we built that first room,

how the whole camp was really a glorified tree house
built by people who were not real sure what they were doing
but never had any doubts about why they were doing it.
Building that camp was a pine and asphalt metaphor
for the building of our family.

And so here I am,
on the roof,
slicing through the tongue and groove roofing boards
so we can strip and reuse the ceiling joists
on some other project.

We continue to look to the future,
to plan on using the lumber
that is still good from the old camp
on some other building,
some other palace for generations well after mine.

I can't help feeling I am a
part of the building I am tearing down.
But I am like an old pine tree,
blown down by wind and age,
nursing a sapling that takes nourishment from
what I leave behind.

THE OBITUARIES PICK-ME-UP

Years ago I started reading the obituaries
to stay up on things.
Occasionally there was a name
that rang a bell,
a parent of a friend
or a college professor from years past.

But now, as I approach my mid 60's,
I turn to the obituaries,
not out of curiosity to see who has died
as much as curiosity to see how old they were.
I don't look at names any more;
I just look for ages.
(It's like checking the stock market.)
The older they were when they went,
the better.

This guy died when he was 84. I've got plenty of time.
This woman died when she was 94. I hope I go before that.
Oh oh. Here's a 67. Well, that still gives me four years.
Whoops, 58. What'd he die of?
Ruptured aorta. Well, you never know.
But, he probably didn't take care of himself.

For the time being, as long as I keep finding people
older than I am,
I'll keep coming back to read these things.
But I know this is a losing game.
As I grow older, the obituaries are going to start
hammering home the message I don't want to hear.
At some point, I'll probably stop reading them.

This growing old thing requires toughness.
I'm working on that.
In the mean time, I'll continue to look for
high numbers.

CLOSING THE DOOR

I stand and look at my emptied office
from the doorway.
I have pondered this moment for years,
wondering what it would be like to walk out
for the last time,
closing the door behind me
and never coming back.

Last week, cleaning out my files felt like
carving off little bits of my being,
throwing away units
and lectures,
and letters of recommendation
that took a good chunk of my life to create
but now,
in the last dwindling hours of my career,
are useless.

But it did give me a chance to reminisce.
There were a few tears,
not because this stuff was going in the waste basket,
but because it brought back memories
of people through the years,
feelings remembered,
relationships ended but not forgotten.

Driving into the school parking lot
my first day as a student teacher
in 1964
I was a nervous wreck.
I sat in the back of Mr. Hanebuth's remedial English class
that morning
as he went over grammar
with kids who couldn't have cared less.

In the middle of the lesson, a young woman entered and handed
him a note.
He looked up at me, said,
"I've got to take care of something,"
gave me the grammar book
and left.

I'd never had so much fun in my life.
I drove home exhilarated.

It's been forty-two years,
teacher and principal,
not entirely stress-free.
But I loved every minute of it.

I will never know if there are any
or how many
kids think of me
as someone who changed their lives.
I like to think there are some.

I've made a difference in the world.
I think it's a little better because I was here.

Someone else is going to sit in this office.
Someone else is going to have the opportunity
to make the lives of children a little better,
to make them believe they can become what they want to be,
that their beauty as people comes from the heart,
not from clothes and straight teeth.

I'm going home now,
taking my pictures and climbing ivy that refuses to die,
my diplomas and Principal of the Year plaque,
the mug full of marbles given to me by the Class of '91,

the pieced-together puzzle portrait of the Class of '95,
the gifts and keepsakes
from kids who wanted me to remember them.

I remember them.

And if I am remembered for anything,
I hope it is for being someone
who cared.

THE MARRIAGE BED

They have kissed their parents goodbye,
moms wiping tears,
dads trying to hold it together.
Alone in the hotel room,
man and wife —
woman and husband,
they climb into bed.

In time, the physical relationship,
which begins as a new adventure,
will diminish in passion and urgency,
But it is in this bed,
when there is darkness outside
and only these two people matter,
that the closeness of their bodies
strengthens the union of their hearts,
and skin on skin acts like an
electric wire,
transmitting strength,
one to the other.

As time goes on,
the love expressed under those sheets and comforters
grows in complexity and intensity.
The two middle aged people
who curl up pressed against each other,
an arm of one draped over the other,
find in that bed a
haven from bills yet to be paid,
jobs that lack satisfaction,
parents who don't want to give up their
homes and cars and independence.

And in the later years,
when the bodies of these two old friends

begin to break down
and there looms on the horizon
the inevitable end of their life together,
they sleep through the night,
hand in hand,
breathing in unison,
certain that the bond that was born
in their marriage bed
will endure beyond the time when one of them does not waken.

SINGING IN THE SHOWER

I don't seem to be able to refrain from singing
when I step into the shower.
Something about the echo-like sound
that my 64-year old vocal chords
produce in that little tiled box
in the corner of the bathroom
tickles me no end.

"I touch your hand and my arms grow strong,
Like a pair of birds that burst in song."

For a while I thought I would never
be able to entertain myself (and my wife)
like that again.

Most people don't know that Parkinson's
can steal away the singing voice—-
limit range, destroy the falsetto,
take the heart out of the music.

I used to be a singer,
church and community choirs and choruses,
community theater;
been King Arthur and Harold Hill and Benny Southstreet
and the Minstrel (..upon a Mattress).
But Parkinson's took that from me.
It was a theft sorely felt.

Then one night,
when I stepped into the shower
for what had become a quiet,
music-free
mundane task,

something prompted me to sing,
not like Curly singing "*Oh, What a Beautiful Morning!*"
but like Ezio Pinza,
rolling my 'r's and rounding my o's,
bringing the sound up from the gut,
holding nothing back,
like Pavarotti carrying "*Nessun Dorma*" over a full orchestra,
not worrying if the noise I was producing could be heard
through three doors and over the sound of the television.

That shower stall worked magic.
My god, I sounded good!
Well, maybe not "good,"
but not bad.

And did I have fun!

That was a long and noisy shower.

I have happily accepted the trade off
of my falsetto
for an ear-splitting but ego-soothing
upper register ending . . . . .

"*Angel and lover, heaven and earth
Am I, with you.*"

followed by

"*When you walk through a storm,
Keep your chin up high,
And don't be afraid of the dark.*"

And I'm not.

THE ROPE SWING

Up in the orchard today by the stone wall
I came across the rope swing
dangling from a limb like a dead grapevine.
It must have been ten years ago
my granddaughters and I
hung that swing.

After I threw the rope over the limb
and knotted it home,
they took turns
climbing higher and higher on the wall
to launch out into the air,
squealing with delight
while I stood by and glowed.

The swing isn't in bad shape—
nylon rope still pretty much intact,
knotted beneath a wooden seat
not yet rotten.

But I can tell it
hasn't been used for years—
a thin layer of lichen on the surface,
a faint green moss on the underside.

Sparkling in its novelty,
it had been a new adventure for them
in a glowing chapter of our past.
But, like a stalk of white phlox that is past
and whose petals are turning,
it's time to cut it down.

WHEN THE CHILDREN LEAVE

We go through the motions when the children leave,
buy special dresses,
rent tuxedos,
hug and kiss strangers
and people we barely know.

But even though we participate
in these celebrations of the future
our hearts are tinged
with melancholy,
a vague awareness of the inexorable momentum
of time's pendulum
that sweeps our little ones out of our arms
and into adulthood,
overwhelming us with the golden weight
of the years gone by.

We were there once.
We know the thrill of independence,
the passion of a new love,
the exhilaration and anticipation of
starting to define who we are as adults
and what we can contribute during our time.
So we join the happy celebrants,
raising toasts, joining the conga line,
pulling out the family albums.

But when the guests leave and the house is empty,
the world is oblivious to our loss,
indifferent to our longing
that they be ours once again.

So we carve
hollow hideaways in our hearts
where we keep forever our little boys
and our little girls
and do not share them
with the world any more
when the children leave.

Conclusions

COMING HOME

Winter is coming.
There's no getting around it.
Springs and summers and autumns behind me,
I am covered in a snow of years.

In the spring of my life,
when I courted Ann,
held our babies,
began my career,
the days were long and getting longer.
Now as I approach the shortening days of winter,
those years seem a mere blink away in time.
And, as we bundle up for the cold,
we marvel at the brevity of the journey.

We are starting to lose friends to the vagaries of age,
presaging the barren forests of winter.
But the budding of the trees
and bursting blossoms,
the summer shade,
the autumn gold —
all have been stunning wrappings of this precious,
gift of life.

We may have figured out
how the human body works,
how a fertilized egg multiplies millions of times,
growing into a human being who breathes
and dreams
and longs for love —
but understanding how
does not eliminate the wonder.

A newborn baby,
a litter of golden retriever puppies,
a nest of garter snakes newly hatched,
a nursing narwhale new to the ocean —
all are miracles.

Like most of us
experiencing the first flurries of winter,
I have been pondering the purpose of this
journey through the seasons.
And so far, the answer
that makes the most sense to me is simply:
Life is a gift to be relished and enjoyed.

Those myriad moments
when a mother looks into the eyes of her week old child,
when a family shares a laugh watching their kitten stalk the dog,
when one living thing connects with the heart of
another living thing,
and through that connection
experiences moments of joy,
even though fleeting —
these are the reasons we are here.

All living things,
human and otherwise,
creatures of the wild
as well as dogs and cats,
young people and old people,
rich and poor
the world over
experience this same joy,
because we are connected,
not only by the blood of life in our veins,
but by the thread of divine love
woven into our being
as part of the miracle of birth.

It is from the source of this loving,
all powerful,
incomprehensible
spirit of creation
that we come as infants in the early spring
and to which we return when
the winter ends.
We have but to look around us for evidence
of this energy that creates and recreates
and infuses life with an urge to create more life,
that is never seen
but is seen everywhere —
in mountain skylines silhouetted against the pink pastels
of a summer sunset,
in the gray twilight of dawn over a silent sea,
in the eyes of tigers,
and sharks
and golden eagles,
in the perishable petals of a rose and dogwood blossom,
in the innocence of puppies and little children,
in the bright warmth of sunshine and
the cleansing power of thunderstorms.

Our world is a cathedral
of statuary
and testimony
and jeweled fabric
and sweet smelling incense
created by an unknowable power,
so enormous
and complex
and intricately interwoven
through everything in the universe
that even the miraculous mind of man
will never fully grasp it.

And so, as the days dwindle down toward the end of the year,
these thoughts reassure me that
something,
albeit unknown to me now,
waits for me when the year has ended.
When that time comes,
perhaps that which is now unknowable
I will see and understand.

But when that time comes
I will be enfolded in the love
that created me and sustained me in life,
and I will realize
I have come home.